THE
GORGEOUS
GEORGIANS
ACTIVITY
BOOK

Terry Deary ✠ Martin Brown

SCHOLASTIC

THE GEORGIAN AGE

The Georgian age was a time when pirates were the scourge of the seas, highwaymen haunted the roads, a crackpot was king and the Americans were revolting ... some things never change! It was also the age of thick make-up, beauty spots, monstrous wigs and padded bosoms – and that was just the men!

In 1714, Queen Anne of the Stuart Family died. George I came over from Germany to take the English throne – he was the first of five kings to rule Britain in the Georgian period. George I wasn't very popular, but the other Stuarts were Catholics and so most Brits didn't want them on the throne. Which pieces complete the portraits of the kings?

| GEORGE I RULED BETWEEN 1714 AND 1727 | GEORGE II RULED BETWEEN 1727 AND 1760 | GEORGE III RULED BETWEEN 1760 AND 1820 | GEORGE IV RULED BETWEEN 1820 AND 1830 | WILLIAM IV RULED BETWEEN 1830 AND 1837 |

1  2 3 4  5  6  7 8  9  10

As king, George I began to make changes. One change was Enclosure, which got rid of a lot of common land (free land which everyone could share). With no land to farm, the peasants had no other choice but to find work in the towns and cities. Can you work out how many peasants are leaving the countryside to find work in the town?

TOWN

There were lots of different people living in Georgian Britain. Daniel Defoe, the author of the book, *Robinson Crusoe*, reckoned there were actually seven classes of people. A maid would have been seen as lower class, while a Lord upper class. Match the numbered speech bubbles with the characters and then decide which order you think Defoe placed them in his class system, from top to bottom.

C 1) I'M A SLAVE-TRADER, SO I'M NOW JOLLY RICH! BY THE WAY, CAN YOU KNOCK DOWN THAT CRUMMY COTTAGE, IT'S SPOILING MY VIEW!

 **D**

2) I'M A COUNTRY PERSON. I USED TO LIVE OFF THE COMMON LAND, BUT NOW I GET WORK WHERE I CAN FIND IT.

B

3) I'M RICH. MY HUSBAND HAS OODLES OF MONEY AND I ENJOY SPENDING IT. WE EVEN HAVE OUR OWN 27-PIECE ORCHESTRA.

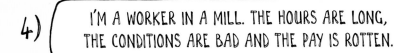

4) I'M A WORKER IN A MILL. THE HOURS ARE LONG, THE CONDITIONS ARE BAD AND THE PAY IS ROTTEN.

 **G**

A

5) I'M POOR AND MISERABLE AND HAVE VERY LITTLE FOOD. I'M SCARED MY CHILDREN WILL STARVE.

6) I'M A MINER WITH FIVE CHILDREN. I'M SO POOR THAT I HAVE TO LIVE IN A CAVE.

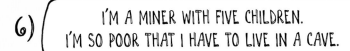

 **F**

E

7) I'M A PARISH PRIEST. I DON'T GET PAID MUCH MONEY, BUT I HAD SALMON FOR DINNER LAST NIGHT. DELICIOUS!

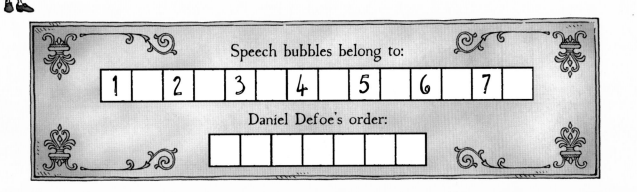

Speech bubbles belong to:

| 1 | | 2 | | 3 | | 4 | | 5 | | 6 | | 7 | |

Daniel Defoe's order:

| | | | | | | |

CHEERLESS FOR CHILDREN

The Georgian age was hard for a lot of people, but it was worse for children. Poor kids were dressed as adults and often worked in foul factories from a very early age.

Would you have survived a Georgian childhood? Here's a quick quiz to find out.

1. One child in three didn't live to be …
a) 3
b) 9
c) 15

2. Careless parents, brothers and sisters could easily take a baby's life. How?
a) They would feed it bad milk and the child would die.
b) They would go to work leaving the baby on its own – the baby would starve.
c) They could roll on top of the baby while they were sleeping and smother them.

IF YOUR FATHER ROLLED OVER HE'D SMOTHER THE LOT OF US!

SNORE

3. Poor families could not afford to keep many children. Where might a parent leave their baby to die?
a) in a car
b) in a drain
c) at the airport

4. Children who had nurses were how many times as likely to die?
a) twice
b) thrice
c) four times

5. In 1741, Thomas Coram opened a hospital for unwanted children. So many were dumped on his doorstep that he couldn't help them all. Roughly, how many died?
a) 100
b) 1,000
c) 10,000

6. Young girls in rich homes had to grow up to be ladies with fine figures. That meant having narrow waists. What object kept their stomachs pulled in?
a) a steel cage
b) a leather belt
c) a whalebone corset

SUCH A FASHIONABLE SHAPE FOR HER FIGURE

AND A FASHIONABLE SHADE OF BLUE FOR HER FACE

7. To keep large numbers of orphans quiet at night, they were …
a) gagged
b) given a mixture full of opium
c) threatened with being sent to the mines if they made a noise

Answers:

1	2	3	4	5	6	7	

Some poor children went to 'dame' schools run by local women, or to 'charity' schools paid for by rich people. Rich parents could afford to send their children to 'public' schools like Winchester. Find the words in CAPITALS in the grid below. The words can be found written up, down, forwards and backwards.

In 1793 there was a 'Great REBELLION' at Winchester school. The BOYS took over a TOWER at the SCHOOL and refused to come down. The GENTLE boys THREW STONES at the teachers below – the not-so-gentle ones FIRED PISTOLS! At the same school in 1818, a pupil rebellion had to be DEALT with by SOLDIERS using … what?

L	O	O	H	C	S	B	G	A
N	O	I	L	L	E	B	E	R
W	E	R	H	T	Y	O	N	S
F	N	E	R	E	W	O	T	Y
I	S	T	O	N	E	S	L	O
R	D	E	A	L	T	T	E	B
E	S	P	I	S	T	O	L	S
D	S	R	E	I	D	L	O	S

NAPOLEON'S CAVALRY IS ONE THING, BUT ARMED ANGRY PUBLIC SCHOOLBOYS ARE QUITE ANOTHER

The letters remaining will spell out the type of weapons the soldiers used.

_ _ _ _ _ _ _ _

One of Winchester's pupils, Thomas Arnold, ended up as head teacher at Rugby School – he wrote the famous book Tom Brown's School Days about life there. But Rugby had its own problems. In 1797, a gang of pupils used gunpowder to blow up the headmaster's door. Which group of pupils do you think did it – group A, B, C, D or E?

FRIVOLOUS FASHIONS

Being a child wasn't much fun, but it was probably worse being a woman! Men expected their wives to be quiet and to obey them. But the worst thing about being a rich Georgian woman must have been the make-up, wigs and clothes they had to put up with.

Imagine you're a Georgian lady getting ready to go to a posh party. Below is a selection of what you might find on your dressing table. See if you can match the product with its use. But beware, two are a deadly poison. Which ones are they?

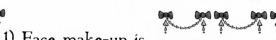

1) Face make-up is ...

2) Silk beauty spots are ...

3) Red Plaster of Paris is ...

4) Black lead eyelashes and false eyebrows made from mouse skin are ...

5) Cork balls are ...

6) Snuff is ...

a) used for lips.

b) held in the cheeks to improve the face.

c) sniffed to clear your head.

d) a flat, white lead paint.

e) stuck on as features.

f) cut out and stuck on to hide scars.

DALMATIANS ARE VERY FASHIONABLE THIS YEAR

CHEESE MADAM?

YUMMY!

YES PLEASE!

By the 1770s, some of the fashions became so ridiculous that it was easy to poke fun at them. A theatre director called Garrick had a character on stage dressed with every kind of vegetable and a _ _ _ _ _ _ dangling from each ear. Colour in the dotted areas to see what Garrick used for earrings.

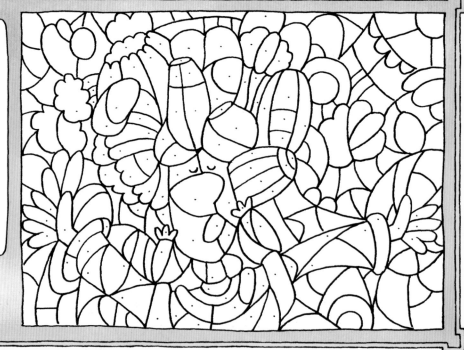

Those fancy fashions and huge wigs were very heavy. To cool themselves down, ladies used fans. They learned to use the fans as a way of flirting. If a lady rested her fan on her lips it meant, 'I don't trust you'; if she half-opened the fan over her face, it meant, 'Someone is watching us.' Using the code below, see if you can match the fan symbols to the alphabet to decode the secret message.

GRUESOME GEORGIANS

Georgian Britain was a prime crime time. In 1822, there were at least 200 hanging crimes. Some experts believed there were as many as 350! Georgians tried to be tough on criminals and held hangings in public so everyone could see what happened to naughty boys and girls.

But the Georgians didn't just hang their criminals, some were deported – sent off to the colonies in smelly ships, while disobedient pirates risked being keel hauled – thrown into the sea and dragged under the bottom of the boat. Punishments varied depending on the crime. Copy the picture boxes into the grid to see what this person's punishment is and why.

1	2	3	4	5
6	7	8	9	10
11	12	13	14	15
16	17	18	19	20

4 — OATS, S / LY A WI

2 — IF / D

5 — HE'S / TCH!

3 — SHE FL / EFINITE

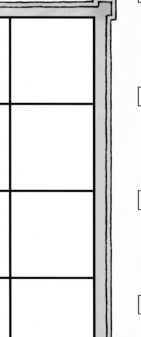

Smuggling was a top crime in Georgian times. Half the tea drunk in Britain at that time was smuggled into the country. In 1748, a man called Chater betrayed a smuggling gang and a law officer called Galley tried to arrest them. Can you add the missing words to find out what happened next?

Missing words not in the correct order:
hunger, groan, middle, rope, stones, nose, bottom, joint, well, pain, torture

They began with poor Galley, cut off his _____, broke every _____ of him and after several hours of _____ dispatched him. Chater they carried to a dry _____, hung him by the _____ to a cross beam in it, leaving him to perish with _____ and _____. But when they came, several days after, and heard him _____, they cut the _____, let him drop to the _____ and threw in logs and _____ to cover him.

Not only did law officers have something to fear in Georgian times, but dead bodies did too! In those days, ruthless villains would steal corpses from graves and sell them to surgeons for research. Would you make a good bodysnatcher? See if you can dodge the law and get your corpse to the surgeon without being caught.

SURGEON

HIDEOUS GEORGIAN HEALTH

Georgian doctors didn't know as much about medicine and the body as we do today. Getting sick was no picnic. You might survive the leeches they used to cleanse your blood, but you may then die of gangrene because the instruments weren't sterilized!

Look at this picture of a sick Georgian gentleman and his doctor. Can you spot nine things that wouldn't have been around in Georgian times?

Those who didn't fancy visiting their doctor took some curious cures for their problems. Can you match the right illness to the right cure?

CURES

A) rub it with the tail of a black cat.

B) bathe in salt water.

I DIDN'T MEAN FOR HIM TO TAKE A BATH IN THE SEA!

ILLNESSES

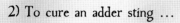

1) To cure a wasp sting …

2) To cure an adder sting …

3) To get rid of of a stye on the eyelid …

4) To relieve swollen joints …

5) To relieve toothache, take a poker, heat it in the fire and …

6) To get rid of a boil on the bottom …

7) To cure bad breath …

8) To cure rabies …

9) Another cure for rabies is to …

C) take a hair from the dog that bit you and swallow it.

D) kill a chicken and place its warm guts over the wound.

NOW HE HAS SMELLY EARS, TOO

E) boil a whole chicken and eat it with six litres of beer.

F) peel the skin off a turnip, roast the pieces and wear them behind the ear.

G) swallow the juice of an onion.

H) stand by a horse, and get someone to tickle it until it kicks the affected area.

I) burn the ear lobe.

DOES THAT FEEL BETTER?

Mentally ill people were called 'mad' and locked away. King George III was one of the mentally ill. One of the treatments that was prescribed was to form blisters on the head then burst them. How many times can you spot the word BLISTER in this grid? The words may run across, up, down, forwards or backwards.

S	I	L	B	L	I	S	T	E	R	E	T	S	I	L	B
I	L	B	L	I	S	T	E	R	E	T	S	I	L	B	L
L	B	L	I	S	T	E	R	E	T	S	I	L	B	L	I
B	L	I	S	T	E	R	E	T	S	I	L	B	L	I	S
L	I	S	T	B	R	E	T	S	I	L	B	L	I	S	T
I	S	T	E	R	E	T	S	I	L	B	L	I	S	T	E
S	T	E	R	E	T	S	I	L	B	L	I	S	T	E	R
T	E	R	E	T	S	I	L	B	L	I	S	T	E	R	B
R	R	E	T	S	I	L	B	L	I	S	T	E	R	E	T

GORGING GEORGIANS

**If Georgians dodged their doctor, they didn't pass up
on a chance to feast! Lots of people still cooked over open fires
as they didn't have ovens. This meant they could roast meat and
boil puddings, but they couldn't bake a cake. Tasty inventions
of the time included toast, chocolate chunks and sandwiches.**

*There were no supermarkets
in Georgian times. Milk was sold
on the streets of cities by milk
maids who carried it around in
open pails. The trouble was the
pails collected unwanted extras!
Unscramble the words in CAPITALS
to read how Tobias Smollet
described them...*

Dirty RAT WE thrown from WOW DINS,
spittle, TONS and tobacco squirts from passersby,
spatterings from coach HE SLEW, dirt and trash
chucked into it by roguish BY SO for the joke's sake,
the spewings of FANS NIT and finally the lice that
drop from the rags of the nasty drab MA WON
that sells this precious mixture.

*Here's a milk maid trying to make her rounds. Can you help her
deliver the milk to the houses from 1 to 10 in the correct order?
Remember, you can't go over the same path twice.*

Besides milk, rich Georgians loved sweets and puddings. Georgians were the first to enjoy raw fruit. With new 'hothouses', they could grow grapes, peaches, pineapples and strawberries. Why not try one of the recipes from that time – strawberry fritters?

STRAWBERRY FRITTERS

YOU WILL NEED:

• 450g large strawberries
(more if you have a lot of friends!)
• 175g plain flour
• 50g caster sugar
• 2 teaspoons grated nutmeg
• 2 eggs
• 225ml single cream
• lard (you can use margarine)

METHOD:

Start this at least two hours before your guests arrive.

1) Dry the strawberries but leave the stalks on so you can hold them when you eat them.

2) Mix the flour, nutmeg and sugar in a bowl.

3) Beat the eggs, stir in the cream and slowly stir the mixture into the flour and sugar.

4) Leave this batter to stand for two hours.

5) Heat some lard in a frying pan. (It's best to get an adult to do this.)

6) Dip each strawberry in the batter – holding it by the stalk.

7) Drop a few strawberries into the hot lard and fry them gently till they are golden brown.

8) Drain them on kitchen towels and keep them warm in an oven while you fry the rest.

9) Eat the strawberries but not the stalks.

10) If you like them, then share them with your friends. If you absolutely adore them, then scoff the lot, describe the taste to your friends and tell them to cook their own!

Georgians also loved cheese. Daniel Defoe, the author of Robinson Crusoe, described a visit to Stilton; 'The cheese is brought to the table with the mites and maggots around it so thick that they bring a spoon with them to eat the mites with, as you do the cheese.' Can you work out how many maggots are infesting this big Stilton?

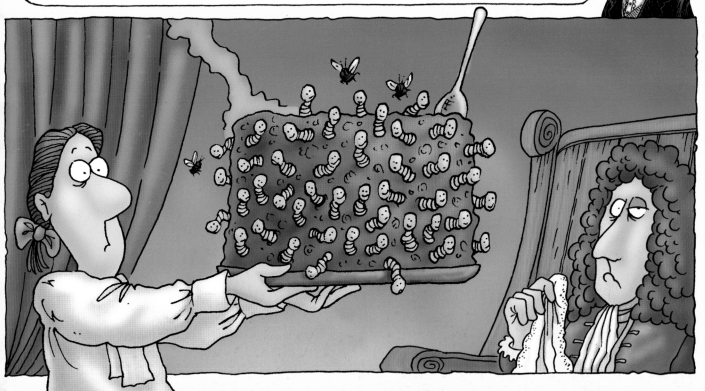

ROTTEN REVOLUTIONS

**While the wealthy were having a good time trying new foods,
law and order was crumbling all around like an over-ripe cheese!
The century of the Georges witnessed bloody revolution in France and
war with the colonies in America, where Britain dumped its convicts.**

The American colonists weren't happy being told what to do or how much tax to pay by a king who was 3,000 miles away. They wanted to make their own decisions. The American War of Independence broke out in 1775, and Britain admitted defeat in 1783. The United States of America was born. Put the following words into the grid below –
CONVICTS, PRESIDENT, USA, TAXES, PARLIAMENT, KING, FREEDOM, REBEL.

Meanwhile, in 1789, poor people in France were unhappy with their king and the high taxes. They rose up and had their revenge on the wealthy aristocrats, by dragging them to an automatic neck-chopper – the guillotine. Which of the following foul facts are true? Answer 'Oui' for yes or 'Non' for no.

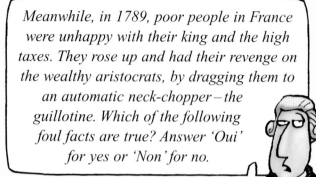

1) The man who designed the French version of the guillotine was Doctor Joseph-Ignace Guillotin.

2) The chopping machine wasn't always called a guillotine. At first it was named a Louisette. Criminals later nicknamed it 'The Widow'.

3) The guillotine's designer said that all the victim felt was a chill on the back of the neck.

4) There was a rule that said French women should be taught about the Revolution. They were encouraged to take their knitting to the executions and watch.

5) The people of Lyon suffered mass guillotine sessions because few people there had supported the Revolution. The guillotine couldn't get through the necks quickly enough, so the revolutionaries brought in good old firing squads to help kill more.

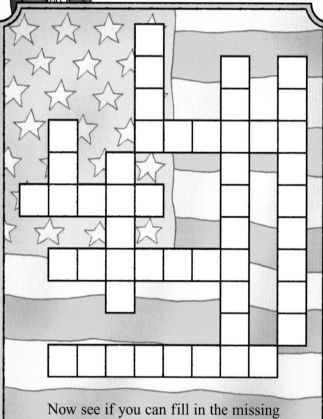

Now see if you can fill in the missing letters to spell the first name of the first president of the United States.

_ _ _ _ _ _ Washington.

One woman who cashed in on the head chopping was Madame Marie Tussaud. She made 'death masks' of the famous. Can you match the chopped heads to the death masks?

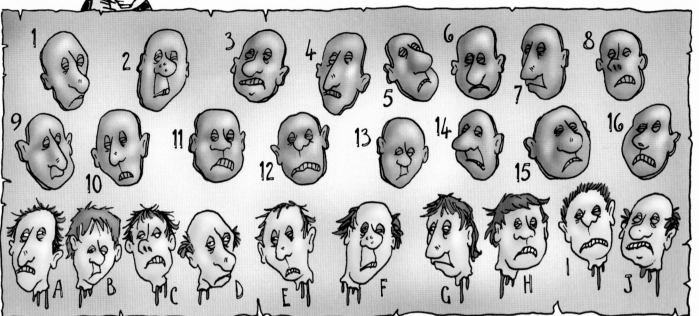

Britain also had its own revolution – the Industrial Revolution. This meant that one man and a machine could do the work of (maybe) ten men. This resulted in nine men losing their jobs. Some of the nine men believed that the answer was to smash up the machine! These machine-smashers were called Luddites because they were said to follow the mighty machine-breaker, Ned Ludd. But who was the real Ned Ludd? Put the pictures in the correct order to find out.

F — AND THEY RAN STRAIGHT OUT THE BACK DOOR. THIS CONFUSED LUDD.
WHERE HAVE YOU GONE?

C — NED LUDD WAS THE VILLAGE IDIOT
NED LUDD IS NO GOOD!
GRR!

D — THE CHILDREN RAN IN THE FRONT DOOR OF THEIR HOUSE
HELP! MUM!
MUM'S GONE TO MARKET!

A — HE COULDN'T FIND THE CHILDREN SO HE TOOK OUT HIS ANGER ON TWO KNITTING FRAMES IN THE HOUSE
NOBODY CALLS NED LUDD NAMES, NOT NOBODY!

B — ONE DAY HE TURNED ON THE TORMENTING CHILDREN
RIGHT! I'M GOING TO BEAT YOU!
EEEK! HE WOULDN'T
LUDD WOULD

E — AFTER THAT NED GOT THE BLAME FOR ANY FRAMES THAT WERE BROKEN – THOUGH HE PROBABLY NEVER BROKE ANOTHER ONE
I SEE NED LUDD'S BEEN HERE

CORRECT ORDER OF PICTURES...

C					

15

HEROES AND VILLAINS

The Georgians had lots of famous heroes, the trouble was that these heroes were actually villains. Remember Robin Hood? He only robbed the rich because the poor didn't have anything! Heroes or villains? You decide.

Probably the most infamous criminal of the time was the highwayman, Dick Turpin, who was reported to have been extremely polite when he held up stagecoaches. Would you have preferred to have been a highwayman or a pirate? Try this board game for two. Choose your role, throw the dice, and, using pennies as counters, see who gets to the treasure first.

YOUR PISTOLS ARE STOLEN! MISS A TURN!

YOU HIDE IN THE MIST AND DODGE THE NAVY! GO FORWARD 2!

YOU DRUNK TOO MUCH RUM AND THE CREW MUTINIES! GO BACK 4!

YOUR SECRET MAP GETS LOST IN A FIGHT! GO BACK TO 1!

THE DENSE TREES HIDE YOU FROM THE SOLDIERS! GO FORWARD 2!

THE NOOSE IS FRAYED – YOU LIVE TO FIGHT ANOTHER DAY! GO BACK 4!

YOU LOSE A PAIR OF PISTOLS IN A GAMBLING GAME! MISS A TURN!

YOU'RE MAROONED ON A ISLAND! GO BACK 4!

YOU ARE RECOGNIZED BY THE COACHMAN! GO BACK TO 1!

YOUR SECRET HIDEAWAY IS DISCOVERED! GO BACK 4!

YOU LOOT A FRENCH SHIP! GO FORWARD 5!

YOU HOLD UP SOME RICH MEN! GO FORWARD 5!

In Scotland, they had Rob Roy MacGregor. To some he was a Scottish Robin Hood. In fact, he was a cattle thief. Draw this picture of Rob Roy. Copy the lines in each square onto the empty grid, then colour it in.

Another villain/hero was the pirate Blackbeard. Earlier pirates used to fly a red flag to frighten their enemies, but in Georgian times, they started to come up with their own designs. How many genuine skull and crossbones flags, like the one below, can you see in this picture?

GOODY, A DIVING BOARD

VISITORS!

GENTLE GEORGIAN FUN

Despite all the fear and violence of the time – or maybe because of it – the Georgians knew how to have a good time. The people of Georgian Britain liked to enjoy themselves in great crowds. Of course, they didn't have televisions to amuse them, or computers, so they packed into parks, thronged theatres and flocked to fairs.

A popular game played by women at fairs was a jingling match. Why not try it with your friends? A class of pupils can play it in a school hall, yard or field.

A JINGLING MATCH

YOU WILL NEED:
• a bell on a string   • 12 scarves

HOW TO PLAY:

1) 12 players are selected.
2) The rest of the class join hands to form a large circle round the 12.
3) One player – the Jingler – has the bell hung round her (or his) neck and her hands tied behind with a scarf.
4) The other 11 players have scarves over their eyes.
5) The blindfolded players try to catch the jingling player who can move anywhere in the circle.

6) If the Jingler escapes for one minute, then he or she wins.
7) If a blindfolded player catches the Jingler, then he or she wins and becomes the Jingler.

Another popular pastime was ballooning – but only for the wealthy. Would you make a good balloonist? See if you can fly across the channel, avoiding all of the hazards.

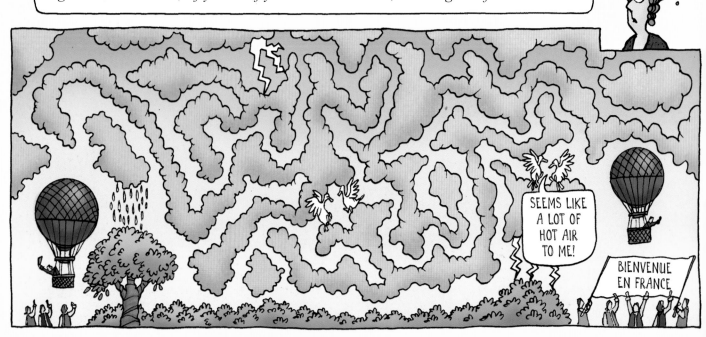

SEEMS LIKE A LOT OF HOT AIR TO ME!

BIENVENUE EN FRANCE

Fair*s were full of freak shows, fire-eaters, acrobats, conjurors and fortune tellers.
Can you spot ten differences between the two pictures and circle them with a pencil?*

GEORGIAN SPORTS AND GAMES

While some Georgians enjoyed 'jingling' and ballooning, others enjoyed more vicious sports. One of the most popular was horse racing, but it could be really cruel. Horses raced time and again in heats as long as four miles.

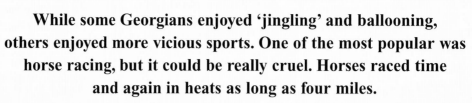

Besides HORSE RACING, there were lots of other popular SPORTS around at the time like FOOTBALL, CRICKET, COCK FIGHTING, BULL and BEAR BAITING, FOX, DEER and HARE HUNTING, RUGBY and BALLOONING. Find the words in CAPITALS in the grid below. The words can be found written up, down, forwards, backwards and across.

C	G	N	I	T	H	G	I	F	G
R	A	E	B	U	L	L	H	O	N
U	C	H	A	R	E	K	B	O	I
S	T	R	O	P	S	E	A	T	N
S	K	C	O	C	T	S	I	B	O
R	A	C	I	N	G	R	T	A	O
Y	B	G	U	R	O	O	I	L	L
F	D	E	E	R	N	H	N	L	L
O	H	U	N	T	I	N	G	E	A
X	S	T	E	K	C	I	R	C	B

The Georgians also liked a simple sport which involved throwing up pebbles and catching them on the back of the hand. The letters remaining in the grid will spell out the name of this sport.

_ _ _ _ _ _ _ _ _ _

The Georgians also enjoyed watching women fight. Add the missing words to read how Cesar de Sassure, a foreign visitor, described one particular fight.

Missing words not in the correct order:
sewn, forehead, coins, Irishwoman, wound, money, fire, weapons, clothing, throat, sword, income, spirits

Both women wore very little _____. One was a stout _____ and the other a small Englishwoman, full of _____ and very nippy. The _____ were a sort of blunt, two-handed _____. Presently the Irishwoman received a cut across the _____ and that put a stop to the first part of the fight. The Englishwoman's supporters threw _____ and cheered for her. During this time the wounded woman's forehead was _____ up, this being done on stage, she drank a large glass of _____ and the fight began again. The Irishwoman was wounded a second time then a third time with a long and deep _____ all across her neck and _____. A few _____ were thrown to her but the winner made a good _____ from the fight.

A newspaper report of 1818 described a Georgian game that went horribly wrong. Some boys were playing in a field where some cows were feeding. One of them suggested that they tie another to the tail of a cow. But the enraged animal dragged the victim up and down the field at full speed. The poor boy was not rescued in time and died. Which boy is going to be dragged by the cow – A, B, C, D or E?

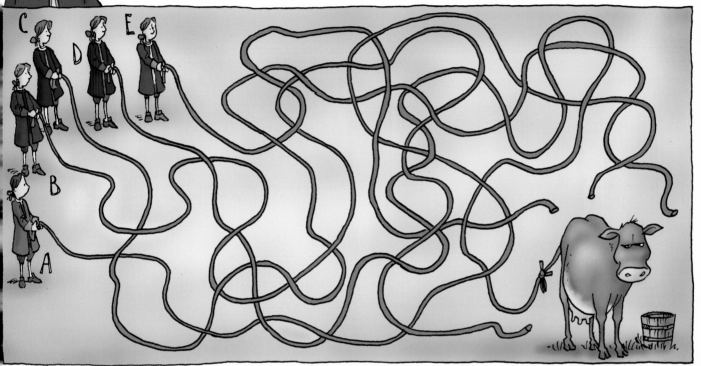

In 1764, a bored lord in Huntingdon invented a game where players had their hands wrapped in bandages, and they had to catch a hen and pull out a feather. How many feathers can you see in this picture?

MAYBE WE SHOULD PLAY IT OUTSIDE NEXT TIME

GORGEOUS GEORGIAN QUIZ

So you think you know a thing or two about the gorgeous Georgians? Test your knowledge with this multiple choice quiz and see if you're a true Georgian expert or not.

1. In 1700 John Asgill went to prison for writing a short book called, *A man can go from here to heaven without … ?*
   a) *dying*
   b) *chocolate*
   c) *a lace cravat*

2. Highwaymen couldn't always afford pistols. In 1774 a Huntingdon highwayman held up a coach using a …
   a) bow and arrow
   b) savage dog
   c) candlestick

THIS IS A CANDLESTICK–UP!

3. What did one Georgian doctor use to pull out rotten teeth?
   a) a penguin
   b) a pelican
   c) a puffin

4. Which of the following would a Georgian gentleman not have worn?
   a) trousers
   b) waistcoats
   c) stockings

5. The Georgians enjoyed watching hounds tearing hares apart. When did this stop?
   a) when the hare waved a white flag
   b) when Queen Victoria was splattered with hare blood in 1899
   c) never

IF THEIR DOG GOT TORN UP, WOULD THEY STILL ENJOY IT?

6. At a 1758 fair one of the attractions was a man eating a chicken. What was so unusual about this?
   a) He ate the whole chicken – guts, feathers and all – and it was alive.
   b) He had just created a new barbecue sauce, and made a fortune by selling it.
   c) The man was a contortionist, and was tied up in ropes and suspended upside down in a crate whilst he ate the bird.

7. The Georgians weren't too keen on foreigners. What did they do to some foreigners on the streets of London?
   a) spat at them
   b) threw dead cats and dogs at them
   c) swore at them in French

ZISS ROTTEN INGLEESH WEZZER, EET'S RAINING

8. Sailors in Nelson's navy suffered bad food. The cheese was often too hard to eat, so what did they do with it?
   a) They used it in mouse traps. The mice broke their teeth on the cheese and starved.
   b) The sailors carved the cheese with their knives to make tough, hard-wearing buttons for their coats.
   c) They used the cheese to play a game like shove-ha'penny on deck. It was called shove cheddar.

9. What useful thing did the watchmaker Andrew Cumming invent in 1775 that we still use today?
   a) a stink trap
   b) roller skates
   c) knickers held up with elastic

BUT AT LEAST HER KNICKERS DIDN'T FALL DOWN

IT WAS HORRIBLE, SHE ROLLER SKATED STRAIGHT INTO THE STINK TRAP

ANSWER PAGES

PAGES 2-3: THE GEORGIAN AGE

In 1714, Queen Anne of the Stuart Family…

Pieces 3 and 5 belong to the portrait of George I; pieces 6 and 10 to George II; pieces 4 and 7 to George III; pieces 1 and 9 to George IV and pieces 2 and 8 to William IV.

As king, George I began to make…

82 peasants are leaving the countryside in search of work.

There were lots of different people living…

1 E   2 A   3 G   4 F   5 B   6 D   7 C

Daniel Defoe's order was G, E, C, F, A, D and B.

Class 1 (G): Most lords managed to earn £5,000 a year – that's about £300,000 today. They enjoyed their money and spent it lavishly on houses, wine and many other things – one lord even had his own orchestra!

Class 2 (E): Some Georgians made their wealth by trading in people. Slavers. They captured Africans, transported them across the Atlantic Ocean and sold the ones that survived. Other Georgians thought that if the local village spoiled their view from their houses, they would knock the village down and move the poor elsewhere.

Class 3 (C): Priests could be poor, but some had some very good parishes and lived very comfortably, eating fine foods like veal and salmon.

Class 4 (F): Even though the work was hard and the pay poor, from the 1790s, tens of thousands flocked to the mills in the towns to find work.

Class 5 (A): Before Enclosure, peasant families used to keep cows, ponies, geese and pigs on the 'common' land. But then the common land was fenced off and sold to rich farmers, so the country people didn't own anything and had to work when the rich farmers wanted them to.

Class 6 (D): A family of seven in Derbyshire lived in a cave. The father was a lead miner and had been born in the cave, so had his five children. The cave was divided into three rooms by curtains.

Class 7 (B): In 1757, a mother and nine children in Buckinghamshire went several days without food.

PAGES 4-5: CHEERLESS FOR CHILDREN

Would you have survived a Georgian…

1 = a   2 = c   3 = b   4 = a   5 = c   6 = a   7 = b

Some poor children went to…

The type of weapon the soldiers used were BAYONETS.

One of Winchester's pupils…

Group D blew up the headmaster's door.

PAGES 6-7: FRIVOLOUS FASHIONS

Imagine you're a Georgian lady getting ready…

1 = d   2 = f   3 = a   4 = e   5 = b   6 = c

Lead was used in Georgian face make-up and eyelashes. Lead is a deadly poison and some symptoms of lead poisoning are twitching, convulsions, muscle soreness, tiredness, weakness, loss of appetite, weight loss, sickness, stomach aches, high blood pressure, confusion, comas and sometimes death!

By the 1770s, some of the…

Garrick used carrots for earrings.

Those fancy fashions and huge wigs were…

The secret message reads, 'Stop flirting with me, or I'll tell your wife!'

PAGES 8-9: GRUESOME GEORGIANS

But the Georgians didn't just hang their criminals…

The woman is being tried for witchcraft. The idea was to throw the suspect into the water to see if they floated. If the woman floated, she was guilty of witchcraft and was taken out of the water and hanged. An innocent person would sink, so would probably drown and die anyway!

Smuggling was a top crime in…

Missing words in the correct order: nose, joint, torture, well, middle, hunger, pain, groan, rope, bottom, stones.

Not only did law officers have…

PAGES 10-11: HIDEOUS GEORGIAN HEALTH

Look at this picture of a sick…

The following weren't around in Georgian times: (1) rubber gloves, (2) syringe (needle), (3) electric scales, (4) electric bedside lamp, (5) digital clock, (6) antibiotics, (7) sticking plasters, (8) hot water bottle and (9) box of tissues.

Those who didn't fancy visiting their doctor…

1 = G   2 = D   3 = A   4 = E   5 = I   6 = H
7 = F   8 & 9 = B, C

Mentally ill people were called 'mad' and…

The word 'blister' can be seen 25 times in the grid.

PAGES 12-13: GORGING GEORGIANS

There were no supermarkets in Georgian times…

Unscrambled words in the correct order: WATER, WINDOWS, SNOT, WHEELS, BOYS, INFANTS, WOMAN.

Here's a milk maid trying to make her…

Georgians also loved cheese. Daniel Defoe…

There are 44 maggots infesting the Stilton.

PAGES 14-15: ROTTEN REVOLUTIONS

The American colonists weren't happy…

The first president of the United States was *George* Washington.

Meanwhile, in 1789, poor…

All are true. That's a lot of ouis!

One woman who cashed in on…

A = 4	B = 13	C = 8	D = 1	E = 10
F = 2	G = 6	H = 11	I = 12	J = 3

Britain also had its own revolution…

The correct order of the pictures is: C, B, D, F, A and E.
The truth is the Luddites never had a leader. Each group was dealt with by the army one at a time and the Luddite riots died as quickly as they had started. If they'd had a single, strong leader it might have been different, but they never had one and they certainly never had one called Ned Ludd – and Ned Ludd was never a Luddite.

PAGES 16-17: HEROES AND VILLAINS

Another villain/hero was the pirate…

There are 6 genuine skull and crossbones flags on the ship.

PAGES 18-19: GENTLE GEORGIAN FUN

Another popular pastime was ballooning…

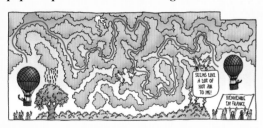

Fairs were full of freak shows, fire-eaters, acrobats…

PAGES 20-21: GEORGIAN SPORTS AND GAMES

Besides HORSE RACING…

The simple sport the Georgians liked was called *Chuckstones*.

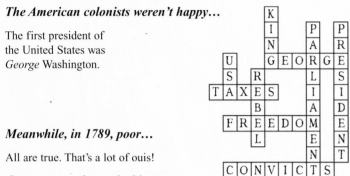

The Georgians also enjoyed watching…

Missing words in the correct order: clothing, Irishwoman, fire, weapons, sword, forehead, money, sewn, spirits, wound, throat, coins, income.

A newspaper report of 1818 described a…

Boy D is going to be dragged by the cow.

In 1764, a bored lord in Huntingdon…

There are 22 feathers in the picture.

PAGE 22: GORGEOUS GEORGIAN QUIZ

1 = a	2 = c	3 = b	4 = a	5 = c
6 = a	7 = b	8 = b	9 = a	

3) A 'pelican' was a tool for pulling out difficult teeth. The instrument got its name because it looked like a pelican's beak.
4) Peasants wore trousers to work in the fields and a gentleman would not be so common as to wear them. Gentlemen wore tighter fitting 'breeches' with stockings.
5) That's right. Hare 'coursing' as it's called is still enjoyed today by many people and many packs of hounds. That's life, hare today, gone tomorrow.
9) A 'stink trap' is a bend in the toilet pipe that stops smells coming up from the drains.

Scholastic Children's Books,
Commonwealth House, 1–19 New Oxford Street,
London WC1A 1NU, UK
A division of Scholastic Ltd
London ~ New York ~ Toronto ~ Auckland ~
Sydney ~ Mexico City ~ New Delhi ~ Hong Kong
Published in the UK by Scholastic Ltd, 2005
Some of the material in this book has previously been published in Horrible Histories:
The Gorgeous Georgians and
The Horribly Huge Quiz Book

Text copyright © Terry Deary, 1998
Illustrations copyright © Martin Brown, 1998
All rights reserved

ISBN 0 439 95903 9

2 4 6 8 10 9 7 5 3 1

The right of Terry Deary and Martin Brown to be identified as the author and illustrator of this work respectively has been asserted by them in accordance with the Copyright, Designs and Patents Act, 1988.

Additional material by Pam Kelt
Additional illustrations and colour work by
Mike Phillips and Stuart Martin

Created and produced by The Complete Works,
St Mary's Road, Royal Leamington Spa,
Warwickshire CV31 1JP, UK

Printed and bound
by Tien Wah Press Pte. Ltd, Malaysia